Flowchart Smart

The ROCK CYCLE

Richard and Louise Spilsbury

Gareth Stevens PUBLISHING

Please visit our website, **www.garethstevens.com**.
For a free color catalog of all our high-quality books,
call toll free 1-800-542-2595 or fax 1-877-542-2596.

Cataloging-in-Publication Data
Names: Spilsbury, Richard. | Spilsbury, Louise.
Title: The rock cycle / Richard and Louise Spilsbury.
Description: New York : Gareth Stevens Publishing, 2019. | Series: Flowchart smart | Includes glossary and index.
Identifiers: ISBN 9781538234761 (pbk.) | ISBN 9781538234778 (library bound)
Subjects: LCSH: Petrology--Juvenile literature. | Geochemical cycles--Juvenile literature.
Classification: LCC QE432.2 S677 2019 | DDC 552--dc23

First Edition

Published in 2019 by
Gareth Stevens Publishing
111 East 14th Street, Suite 349
New York, NY 10003

Produced for Gareth Stevens by Calcium
Editors: Sarah Eason and Harriet McGregor
Designer: Emma DeBanks
Picture researcher: Rachel Blount

Picture credits: Cover: Shutterstock: Seveniwe (br), Smartha (c); Inside: Shutterstock: Corlaffra: pp. 18–19; T. Dallas: pp. 30–31; Djelen: p. 41t; Fairy-N: p. 4tl; Flegere: pp. 40–41; Khadi Ganiev: pp. 34–35; Mark Godden: p. 18b; Kamieshkova: p. 4cr; LesPalenik: p. 27; Linnas: p. 21b; Juan Carlos Alonso Lopez: p. 31t; Macrovector: pp. 36–37; Maksimilian: pp. 8–9; Maridav: p. 33b; Mopic: pp. 6–7; Vladimir Mulder: p. 7b; Nahlik: p. 15t; Nikolas JKD: pp. 4–5; Perutskyi Petro: p. 13t; Photopictures: p. 26; Trum Ronnarong: p. 44; Sementer: pp. 14–15; Serjio74: pp. 1, 24–25; Smartha: p. 8bl; Sombra: p. 23b; Chainarong Suriya: p. 39t; Mr. Rawin Tanpin: p. 35t; Tom Tietz: pp. 32–33; Valentin Valkov: pp. 38–39; Vvoe: pp. 4b, 28–29; WeAre: p. 45; Kris Wiktor: p. 24b; www.sandatlas.org: pp. 12–13; YuRi Photolife: pp. 20–21.

Printed in the United States of America

CPSIA compliance information: Batch #CW19GS: For further information contact Gareth Stevens, New York, New York at 1-800-542-2595.

Contents

Chapter 1 **Rocks Rule!** 4

Chapter 2 **Igneous Rock** 12

Chapter 3 **Sedimentary Rock** 18

Chapter 4 **Metamorphic Rock** 24

Chapter 5 **Rocks Under Attack** 30

Chapter 6 **Using Rocks and Minerals** 38

Glossary 46

For More Information 47

Index 48

Chapter 1

Rocks Rule!

The ground on which we stand, walk, and live is made from rocks. These rocks form the solid **crust**, or outermost layer of our planet. If you go down deep enough underwater you see that they also form the bottom or floor of the seas and oceans of the world.

All of the rocks on Earth are made up of **minerals**. Minerals are solid substances that form naturally in the ground. They are the building blocks of rocks. Different rocks are made up of different combinations of minerals. Granite rocks are made up of different colored minerals called feldspar, mica, and quartz. Limestone rocks mostly contain the mineral calcite. There are about 2,500 known minerals.

The pink color in this granite rock is feldspar. Feldspar is a common mineral that is found in almost all types of rock.

Minerals are made from **elements**, which are the simplest of all chemical substances. A mineral may be a single element, such as copper or gold, or it may be made up of a number of elements. Different elements combine in different ways and they are one reason we get different types of minerals and rocks. They differ in hardness, color, sheen, and streak (the color when a mineral is ground to a powder). Some also form in regular repeating shapes called crystals.

Meteorites have made huge craters like this one. Most meteorites contain several minerals including metal and silicate minerals.

Get Smart!

Most rocks form from minerals from Earth, but some rocks come from space! These are called meteorites. Their elements and minerals may be different to those found in Earth rocks. They are mostly made of metal, usually iron. In the past, meteorites crashed through Earth's **atmosphere** and landed on Earth, leaving giant holes called craters in some places on the planet.

Minerals from Earth

Most of the rocks on Earth form deep within the planet, where it is intensely hot. To understand how rocks form and change we need to understand what is going on deep beneath our feet.

Earth is like an onion, composed of different layers. The crust layer of hard rock is only about 25 miles (40 km) thick. Below the crust is a layer of hot rock called the **mantle**, which is 1,800 miles (2,900 km) thick and mostly made from silicate minerals, from the element silicon. The mantle is around 1,832° F (1,000° C) near the crust, but increases to 6,692° F (3,700° C) near Earth's ball-shaped **core**. The **pressure** in Earth's core is very great. It is caused by the weight of all the rock above pushing downward.

The core consists of two parts: an outer layer of **molten** rock and a solid inner core, mostly made up of iron. The inner core is as hot as the surface of the sun: about 10,830° F (6,000° C). This heat makes molten rock, called **magma**, rise up toward Earth's surface. As magma rises, it cools. As it cools, different minerals inside it combine to form new minerals that can later harden and become rocks.

The core is about 1,802 miles (2,900 km) below Earth's surface and has a radius of about 2,165 miles (3,485 km).

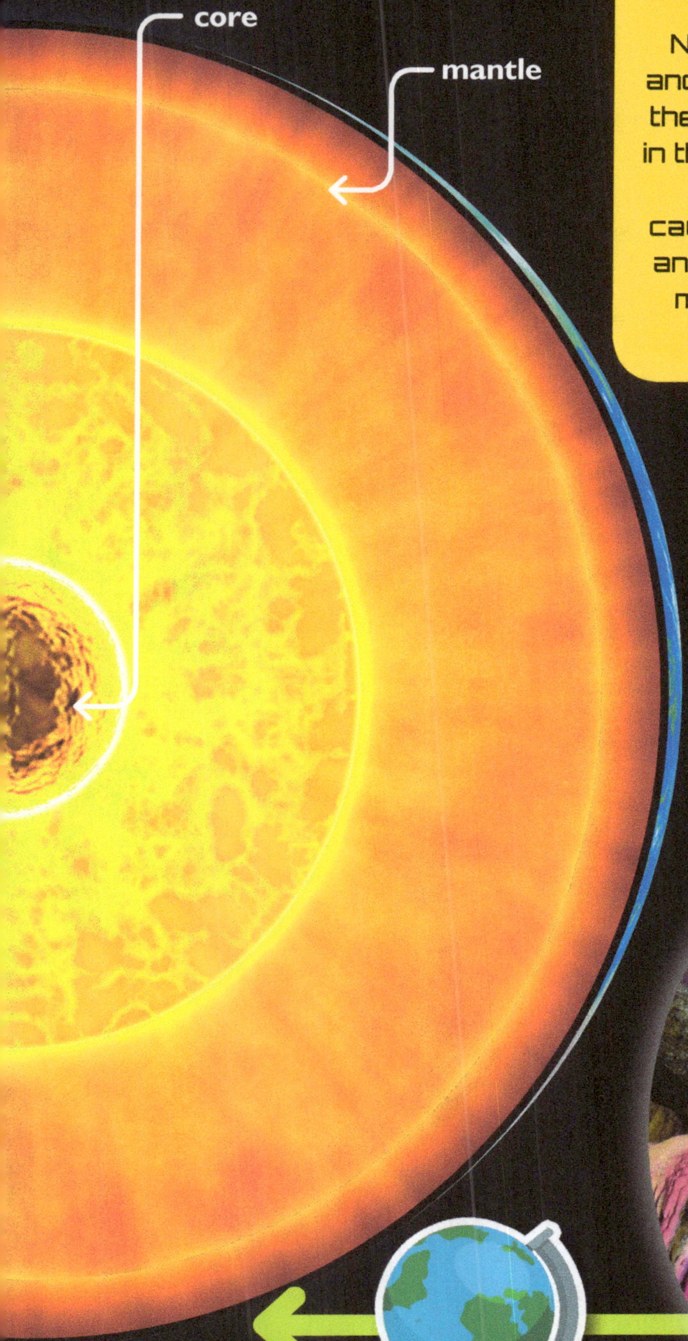

Get Smart!

New minerals can form when rain and seawater soak into the ground. If they sink far enough through cracks in the crust that they meet hot mantle rock, they heat up rapidly. This causes the hot water to break down and mix with some of the rock in the mantle. Later, as the water cools again, new minerals form.

As mineral-rich water drips into caves it forms new minerals in **stalactites** like this. These look purple because they are artificially lit.

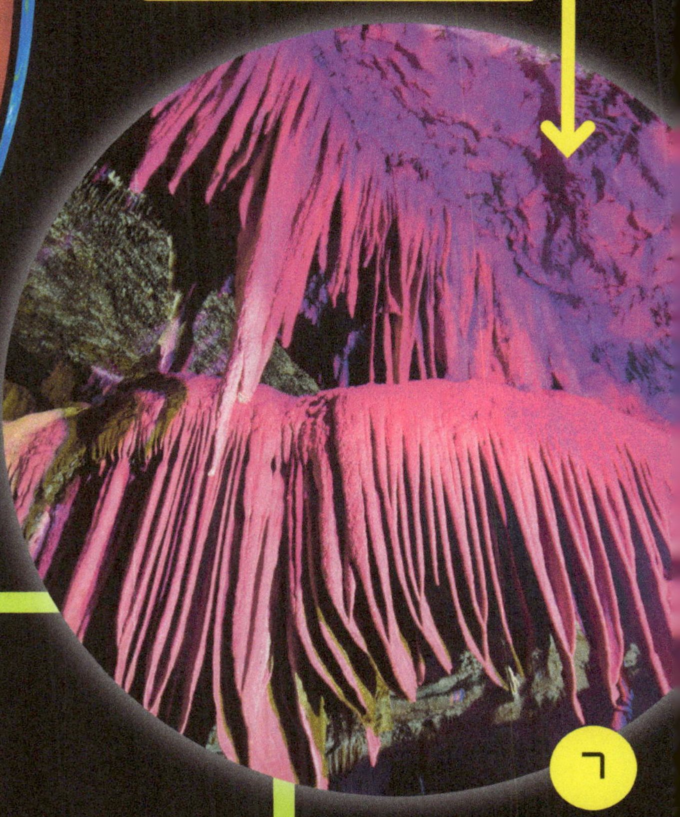

Recycling Rocks

Earth's rocks are constantly changing as they go through a process called the **rock cycle**. Over periods of millions of years, the same rocks are **recycled**. They are formed and then they are either changed into new types of rock or broken down into pieces. The tiny pieces can also eventually form new rock.

Scientists usually **classify** rocks by how they were made or formed. There are three major types of rocks: **metamorphic**, **igneous**, and **sedimentary**. Igneous rocks form from magma. The magma rises up from the mantle toward the surface and sometimes erupts as hot, liquid rock from **volcanoes**. On Earth's surface, the liquid rock cools and becomes solid. It is then broken down by **weathering** and **erosion**, and eventually makes up the soil that fills our fields and yards.

Sedimentary rocks form from compressed, or squashed, layers of these small grains, or **sediment**. When sedimentary rock sinks deep below Earth's surface, it is heated by magma and compressed by other rock layers weighing down on it from above. This changes the sedimentary rock into metamorphic rock. Later, under extreme heat, the metamorphic rock melts and the whole recycling process begins again.

The ocean waves smash against the pebbles along a shoreline. This helps break them down into smaller and smaller pieces.

In the rock cycle, each type of rock can be changed into another type of rock. The full rock cycle takes millions of years.

Get Smart!

If you walk along a coastline, you may come across stones and pebbles of many different colors and types. Some of the pebbles will be from rocks worn away nearby. Others are carried there by the ocean from rocks far away. As the waves rub the pebbles against one another they become smaller and smaller, until they become grains of sand or sediment.

Get flowchart smart!

Understanding the Rock Cycle

Follow the steps in this flowchart to understand how the rock cycle works.

Igneous rocks form from the magma that rises up from the mantle toward Earth's surface.

Later, under extreme heat, the metamorphic rock melts and the whole recycling process begins again.

Flowchart Smart

Over time, igneous rocks slowly break down into smaller pieces and grains, called sediment.

Over millions of years, sedimentary rock forms as layers. The upper layers of rock squash any water from the lower layers of rock, until they become cemented together.

When lower layers of sedimentary rock are heated by magma, they change again, this time into metamorphic rock.

Chapter 2

Igneous Rock

The word igneous means made from fire or heat. The rock cycle starts when rocks underground are heated so greatly that they melt to form magma. Sometimes, enough pressure builds up to force the magma upward from deep inside Earth. It may then cool and solidify within the crust, or sometimes it can erupt suddenly from a volcano.

When magma erupts onto Earth's surface from a volcano we call it lava. In the cool air above the ground, this red-hot lava cools down and hardens and forms new rock. These types of rocks are called igneous rocks.

The exact type of igneous rock formed from lava depends on what minerals are in it. One of the most common types of igneous rock is granite. It is formed when magma cools slowly. Other types of igneous rock include obsidian and basalt, which form when magma cools more quickly.

Pumice is a type of igneous rock that is created during volcanic explosions.

Lava burns everything in its path as it moves across land.

Get Smart!

We make glass in roughly the same way that igneous rocks form. To make glass, you must heat a mixture of minerals (mainly silica in the form of sand) to very high temperatures. When it cools quickly, it hardens to become glass. Obsidian is a type of natural glass formed by volcanoes.

Crystals

Crystals are rocks that form solid structures with definite shapes including flat sides, sharp edges, and corners. Most crystals form when hot magma from inside the mantle rises and cools. Some crystals are small, like the crystals that you sometimes see inside a piece of granite rock. Other crystals are huge.

Certain minerals form crystal shapes within magma. Diamonds are crystals that formed up to 100 miles (160 km) under Earth's surface, deep inside the mantle. The heat and the pressure of the weight of all the rock above the minerals melts carbon and forms tough diamond crystals. We find diamonds at Earth's surface because as magma rises to the surface it carries the crystals with it from the mantle where they first formed.

The word crystal comes from Greek words that mean "icy cold" because in the past people thought crystals were ice that never melted.

Crystals need space to form. Some crystals form when minerals mix with water underground. The liquid full of minerals seeps into cracks that run along inside layers of rock. As it cools and hardens, the minerals form crystals. This is how veins or channels of quartz crystal form inside other rocks. Some crystals form inside gaps in rocks. A **geode** is a hollow in a rock that has an inner layer of crystals on it. When mineral-rich water soaks through an air bubble, some minerals remain in the bubble and form crystals.

This is the Giant's Causeway, in Ireland. It is so-named because in ancient times, people could not explain the basalt columns seen here, so a legend grew that they were the remains of a causeway built by a giant.

Get Smart!

The Giant's Causeway is an area on the coast of Northern Ireland where there are about 40,000 columns of crystallized basalt rock, left there after a volcanic eruption long ago. The columns formed inside a lava flow as it cooled very slowly but very evenly. Most of the columns are hexagonal, although some have four, five, seven, or eight sides. The tallest are about 40 feet (12 m) high.

Get flowchart smart!

How Igneous Rock Forms

Follow this flowchart to take a look at how igneous rocks are formed.

Rock is heated up deep underground. The rock turns into a liquid—magma.

Pressure forces the magma upward.

The magma cools further and hardens. In its hard form it becomes a rock—igneous rock.

As magma nears Earth's surface, it begins to cool.

Magma may erupt from a volcano or it may turn to a solid in Earth's crust as it cools.

Flowchart Smart

Chapter 3

Sedimentary Rock

The formation of sedimentary rocks is different from the formation of igneous rocks. They look and behave very differently, too. Sedimentary rocks also hold exciting secrets that tell us about Earth's history and the plants and animals that lived on Earth long ago.

The rocks on Earth's surface are under constant attack. They are worn away by wind, rain, ice, and snow. The little pieces of sediment that fall off them are washed or blown into rivers, lakes, and the oceans. Once they are washed into waterways, the sediment sinks to the bottom. Over millions of years, the weight of layers of sediment higher up squashes the lower layers. Water trickling through also **deposits** minerals that gradually help cement the pieces of sediment together. These two processes turn the sediment into solid sedimentary rock.

Limestone is a crumbly type of sedimentary rock that formed mainly from the tiny broken remains of dead sea animals.

Most sedimentary rocks are made up of many layers or bands of rock, often of different colors. These layers are called **strata**, and formed at different times from pieces of sediment that were worn away from different rocks or carried to the site by rain or rivers. Each layer contains pieces of sediment of different minerals of different colors and sizes. This is why the layers of rock vary in their appearance.

These sedimentary rock layers are part of the Summerville formation in Utah.

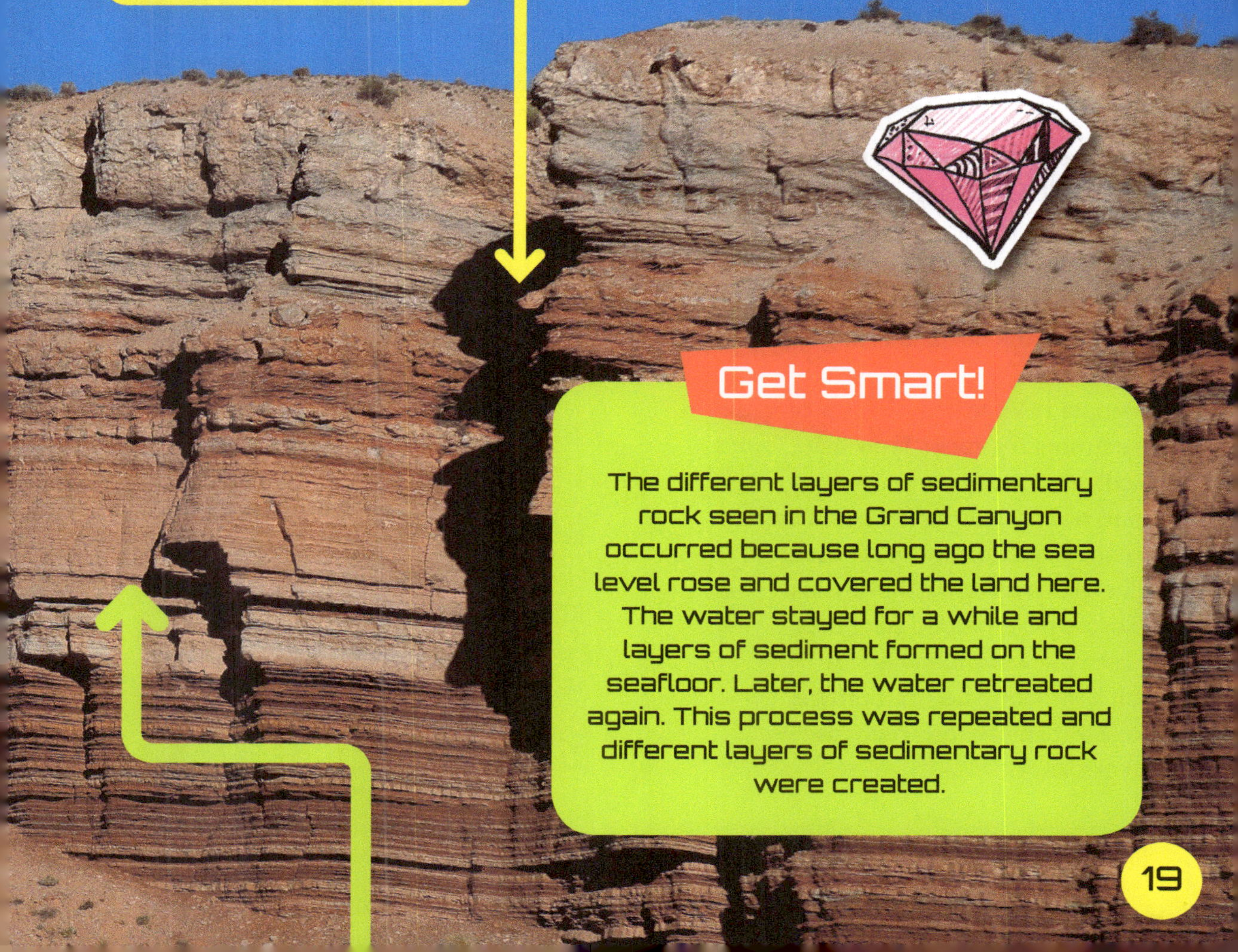

Get Smart!

The different layers of sedimentary rock seen in the Grand Canyon occurred because long ago the sea level rose and covered the land here. The water stayed for a while and layers of sediment formed on the seafloor. Later, the water retreated again. This process was repeated and different layers of sedimentary rock were created.

Fossils

Fossils are the remains of plants and animals that lived millions of years ago and are now **preserved** in rock. Fossils are commonly found in sedimentary rocks due to the way that these rocks form. Unlike most igneous and metamorphic rocks, sedimentary rocks form at temperatures and pressures that do not completely destroy the plant and animal remains.

The majority of the world's fossils are of sea animals that had shells. When a sea animal died and sank to the seafloor, the soft parts of its body quickly rotted away. The shell that was left behind was gradually buried under layers of sediment. Over hundreds of thousands of years, water with tiny pieces of sediment **dissolved** in it soaked into the shell. Gradually, minerals from the water replaced the minerals that made up the shell. The minerals turned into rock that was exactly the same shape as the shell, creating a fossil.

People have found all sorts of fossils in sedimentary rock. They have found individual body parts, such as teeth and bones, and have been able to piece together entire dinosaur skeletons using fossil remains. Fossils have helped scientists discover what life was like on Earth long before humans existed and before records were kept.

This is a fossil of a type of ancient flying creature called a pterosaur, which lived on Earth around 200 million years ago.

Get Smart!

In 2017, a fossil of a plant-eating dinosaur was discovered in Patagonia, South America. It is thought to be one of the largest dinosaurs to walk the planet. *Patagotitan mayorum* would have weighed more than 10 African elephants. Its thighbone was taller than most adult men. The researchers who studied the 100-million-year-old fossils say the dinosaur likely weighed more than 70 tons (63 t) and was more than 120 feet (36 m) long.

Ammonites, types of sea snails with ribbed and spiral-shaped shells, are among the most widely known fossils.

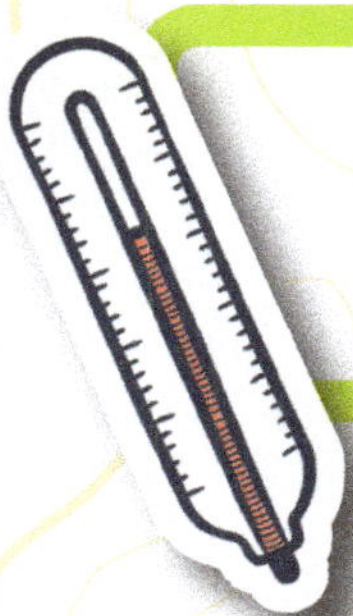

Get flowchart smart!

How Fossils Form

Follow the flowchart for a closer look at how fossils form.

A sea animal dies and its body sinks to the seafloor.

Minerals from the water replace the minerals that make up the shell and turn into rock that is exactly the same shape as the shell, creating a fossil.

Flowchart Smart

Gradually, the soft parts of the animal's body rot.

The hard part of the animal's body—the shell—becomes buried under layers of sediment.

Over hundreds of thousands of years, water with tiny pieces of sediment dissolved in it soaks into the shell.

Chapter 4

Metamorphic Rock

Metamorphic is a word that comes from two Greek words that mean "change form." Metamorphic rock is created deep inside Earth where the intense heat and pressure can break down and completely change the form and makeup of sedimentary or igneous rocks to form new metamorphic rocks.

Over millions of years, layers of sedimentary rock build up in rivers, lakes, and seas. As more and more layers build up, one on top of the other, the older layers at the bottom of the pile are forced deeper into Earth. The deeper they sink, the closer they get to the intense heat of the mantle, and to hot, molten magma.

In some places, heat generated inside Earth warms underground water so greatly that it bursts out of the ground in hot geysers like this one.

The intense heat and the weight of the rock in the crust above pressing down on the sedimentary rock breaks down the minerals in it to form new minerals. Water may pass over the rock, dissolving and removing some of the original minerals in the rock. It may also deposit other minerals that were dissolved in the water. As this new combination of minerals bakes and mixes together it forms a new metamorphic rock. Slate and marble are two types of metamorphic rock.

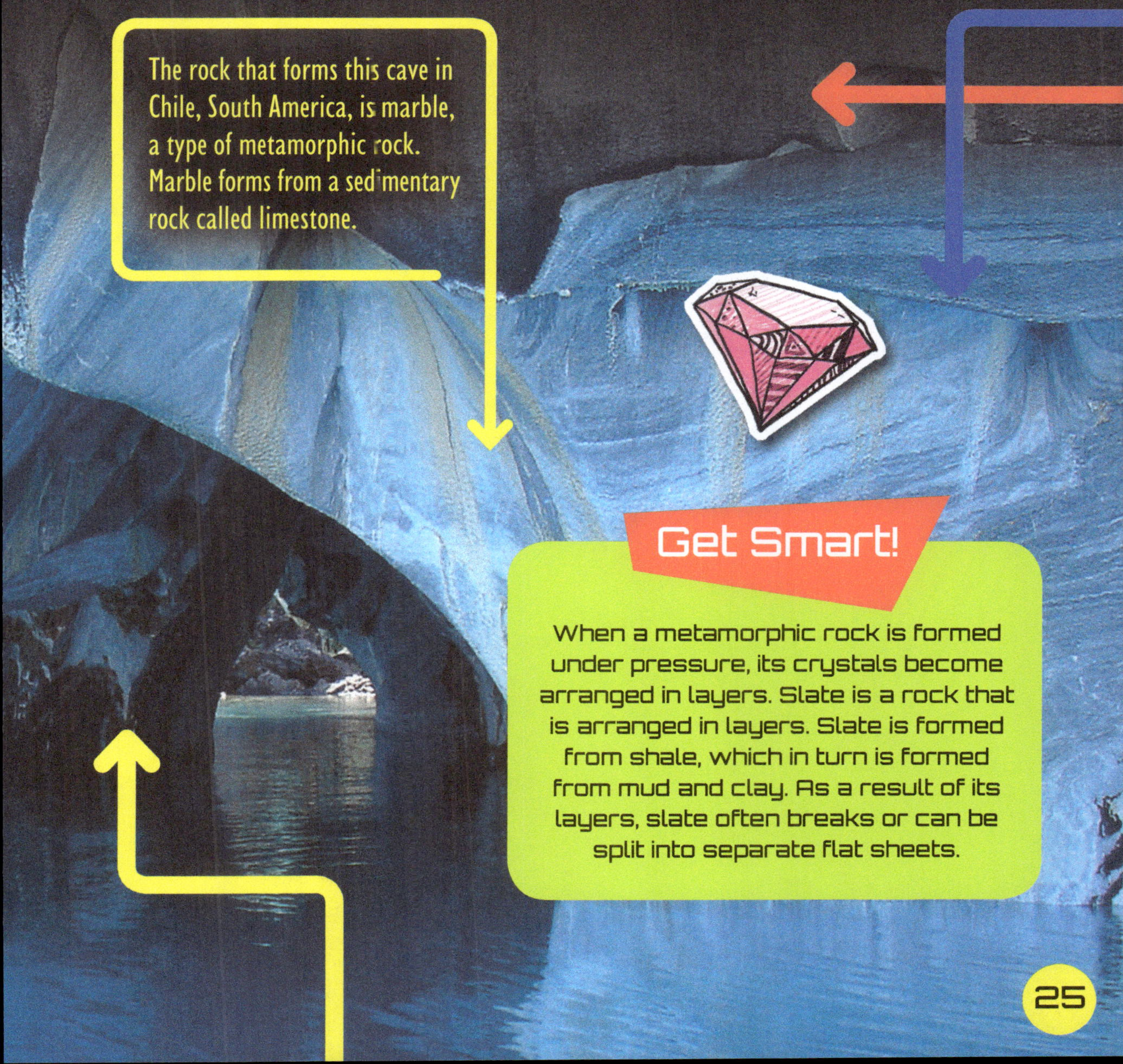

The rock that forms this cave in Chile, South America, is marble, a type of metamorphic rock. Marble forms from a sedimentary rock called limestone.

Get Smart!

When a metamorphic rock is formed under pressure, its crystals become arranged in layers. Slate is a rock that is arranged in layers. Slate is formed from shale, which in turn is formed from mud and clay. As a result of its layers, slate often breaks or can be split into separate flat sheets.

Reaching the Surface

If metamorphic rocks develop deep inside Earth, how do they reach the surface? Metamorphic rock can change into igneous or sedimentary rock. If heat inside Earth melts metamorphic rock, it can become igneous rock and may reach the surface through a volcano. Another way metamorphic rock can reach the surface is by the movement of Earth's **tectonic plates**.

Earth's crust is not one complete piece. Over time, it has cracked in places to form giant rafts of rock called tectonic plates. These plates float on top of the mantle. The mantle moves very slowly and as it does so it moves the plates, too. When tectonic plates move against each other, one plate sometimes pushes under another plate. Other times, two plates may push more equally against each other and the edges where they meet are forced upward.

A fault like this one in Earth's crust is caused by the movement of tectonic plates. As plates move, the rocks at the surface can break.

Gneiss is a metamorphic rock that was twisted into bands by great pressure inside Earth.

These movements of the crust can force rock that was once deep below the surface higher up and even to the surface. These movements can even create mountains and lift rocks that were once part of a seabed high above sea level. So, metamorphic rock from within planet Earth can gradually make its way to the surface or close enough to the surface that humans can dig down and get it.

Get Smart!

Some metamorphic rocks have zigzag lines running through them. That is because Earth's crust moves slowly over the hot layer of mantle below it. As the lower layers of the rocks in the crust move over the mantle, the extreme heat and pressure from the rocks above twist and shape new metamorphic rock as it forms.

Get flowchart smart!

How Metamorphic Rocks Form

Follow the flowchart to see how metamorphic rock forms.

As more and more layers of sedimentary rock build up, the older layers at the bottom of the pile are forced deeper into the planet.

As this new combination of minerals bakes and mixes together, it forms brand-new metamorphic rocks.

Flowchart Smart

As lower layers of rock sink deeper, they become hotter as they move closer to the intense heat of the mantle inside Earth.

The heat and the weight of the rock in the crust above softens, breaks, and bakes the rock.

Water dissolves and removes some of the original minerals in the rock. It also deposits new minerals in the rock.

Chapter 5

Rocks Under Attack

Weather has a huge effect on rock, and weathering can change rock types from one to another. This, too, is part of the rock cycle.

Different types of weather can wear away the surface of rocks, breaking them down into smaller and smaller pieces. Most of us have felt the force of a strong wind as it blasts against us. Wind can blast rock surfaces and when it carries sand along with it, the grains of sand can rub and grind away the rock. When it rains, water moves into gaps in rock surfaces. If the water freezes into ice, it expands and takes up more space. This forces the crack in the rock to open and breaks off pieces.

Weathering can hollow out holes across large areas of rock.

Fast-moving river water can carry rocks with it. The rocks rub against the riverbed and wear it away. When winds whip up strong waves, the waves pound against rocks on the shore, splitting apart tiny cracks so that pieces of rock fall into the sea. The waves also carry other rocks and stones and send them crashing into coastal rock with great force. This breaks up the coastal rocks and wears them away.

High winds at sea whip up strong waves and increase the weathering of rocks.

Get Smart!

When gases and smoke from vehicles, factories, and power plants get into the air, they can mix with rainwater and make it acidic. This is known as acid rain. Acid rain can dissolve some minerals in rocks and damage and break up the rock surfaces.

Erosion

Like weathering, erosion also plays a big part in the rock cycle. Water, wind, and ice all cause erosion and carry weathered pieces of rock to new places.

How the different pieces of rock are moved depends on their size. Tiny grains of rock, such as sand, are light enough that they can be blown to a new place by the wind. Larger and heavier fragments of rock may be washed away from their parent rock by rainwater or a flood. Fast-flowing rivers have more power and can transport large rocks, but slow-moving rivers can only transport small pieces of rock.

This wind and sand-blasted arch is in Arches National Park, Moab, Utah.

At an ocean shore, the waves erode the rock and carry away the pieces that break off. Some are carried long distances across the sea. Coastal erosion is worse when extreme weather such as a hurricane hits the shore. As pieces of rock are carried along by the water, they also knock against one another. They gradually wear away and become smaller and smaller. Eventually, rivers and waves deposit grains of rock somewhere new.

Get Smart!

When rocks are weathered and eroded into tiny grains, they are known as sediment. Sediment can wash into seas and oceans and sink to the seabed. There it forms layers that eventually develop into new sedimentary rock.

This land has been eroded by glaciers. These huge chunks of ice moved slowly across the land and created mountains.

Soil

Soil is the layer of dirt we see in our backyards, parks, and fields and in which trees and other plants grow. It might surprise you to know that one of the main ingredients of soil is rock.

It takes a very long time for weathering and erosion to wear away rocks into smaller and smaller pieces. A hard rock, such as granite, takes 10 times longer than a soft rock, like limestone, to wear away. Eventually, the rocks are broken down into tiny pieces and carried onto an area of land where they begin to form soil.

Tiny pieces of rock and minerals are not the only ingredients of soil. Soil contains rocks and minerals, air, water, and organic matter (substances that are or were once alive). Plants grow between the grains of rock. Their roots open up spaces between the grains of rock where water and air get in. Tiny animals start to live among the grains. The plants drop dead leaves and animals produce waste. When the plants and animals die, they also add nutrients to the soil. Nutrients are chemicals that other plants and animals can use to grow and live. The organic matter also helps bind the soil together.

Scientists examine sections of soil to discover the rocks and minerals it contains. There are different types of soil around the world, all made up of different rocks and minerals.

Get Smart!

Crops and other plants grow well on the soil that surrounds a volcano. That is because the ash that falls down after an eruption is made up of minerals from igneous rock. The minerals in the ash join other minerals on the land to form a rich, dark soil in which crops thrive.

Looking at a cross-section through soil, we see that the top layer where plants grow has the finest grains and the soil sits on a layer of solid rock below.

Get flowchart smart!

How Soil Forms

Follow the steps in this flowchart to find out how soil forms.

Different types of weather wear away the surface of rocks, breaking them down into smaller and smaller pieces.

Water, wind, and ice cause erosion and carry the weathered grains of rock to new places.

The nutrients, air, and water in the soil encourage more plants and animals to live in it and enrich it further.

Layers of rock grains and minerals build up and plants start to grow in them.

↓

Water and air fill spaces between the rock grains.

↓

Plant and animal waste and organic matter add nutrients to the soil and help bind it together.

Flowchart Smart

Chapter 6

Using Rocks and Minerals

The rock cycle provides us with the things we rely on every day. We need the rock cycle to create the soil we grow plants in. We rely on the minerals from weathered rocks that are in our food, such as iron, to grow and keep healthy.

Without the rock cycle, we would not have **fossil fuels**. The gasoline that powers automobiles and other vehicles, and the electricity that powers other machines, comes from fossil fuels. Fossil fuels are coal, oil, and natural gas. They formed from ancient plant and animal remains as part of the rock cycle. The pressure that pushed down to create rock also helped turn the remains into fuels.

The grains of rock in soil provide nutrients that plants need. Nitrate minerals provide nitrogen, which helps leaves grow. Potassium-containing minerals help plants fight disease.

The rock cycle helps us in other ways, too. Builders and engineers use rocks to construct buildings, streets, bridges, and tunnels. Quartz from sand is used to make glass. Grains of rock are mixed with sand and cement to make concrete, and with tar to make street surfaces. Slate is used for roof tiles because it is strong and long-lasting but it also splits easily into tiles.

This concrete floor is being cut with a diamond-coated blade. Diamonds form during the rock cycle and are the hardest known substance.

Get Smart!

There is a huge range of uses for crystals. Some are so rare and beautiful they are called gemstones and are sold to make jewelry. We eat salt crystals that come from underground hard rock salt. Quartz crystals in watches help keep time. Machines such as DVD players and laser scalpels (knives) all contain crystals. The list is seemingly endless.

Metal Matters

Rocks contain metallic minerals that are especially useful to us. The way we use metals depends on the properties of the metals, such as whether they are shiny, hard, or tough.

The metal aluminum is easy to shape, lightweight, and does not rust like iron. So it is used to make soda cans, and automobile and aircraft parts. Copper is a metal through which electricity easily flows so it is used to make electric cables. Steel is used to construct giant tankers and other large ships because it is very strong for its weight.

Copper is one of the most abundant minerals found on Earth's surface. It is extracted from its **ore** before it is used.

Rocks that contain metals or minerals in large amounts are called ores. To get a metal such as gold from its ore, it needs to be separated from all the other minerals in the ore. First, the rocks are dug up from the ground, usually in a mine. Then the ore is ground up and crushed into pieces. Then poisonous salt called cyanide is added to it. This causes a change that makes the gold **soluble**. As the gold is now soluble, it can move through a fine filter, leaving behind the other minerals in the ore. Then carbon is dipped in the gold solution to make the gold form clumps that can easily be separated from the cyanide.

Hot, melted liquid metal can be poured into molds to make different-shaped objects when the metal cools and hardens.

Get Smart!

Gold is a precious metal because it is rare, shiny, and beautiful to look at. As well as being used to make jewelry, a thin layer of gold is used on the visor of an astronaut's helmet to filter out the sun's harmful rays.

Get flowchart smart!

Making Gold

Follow the steps in this flowchart to understand how we get gold metal from its ore.

Ore containing gold is dug up from the ground in a gold mine.

Carbon is dipped into the gold solution to make the gold form clumps that can easily be separated from the cyanide.

Flowchart Smart

The ore is crushed into pieces.

Poisonous salt called cyanide is added to the gold to make it soluble.

The soluble gold drips through a fine filter, leaving behind the other minerals in the ore.

Rocks and Us

The rock cycle is incredibly important in our lives but it is a very slow and gradual process. It takes millions of years for minerals to form new rocks. It is sensible to make sure that we do not damage or waste them so that we have enough for the future.

One way to reduce the amount of minerals we use is to buy less. Think twice before replacing a cell phone, for example. Another way is through recycling. Cars can be crushed so the steel they were built from can be reused. Aluminum and steel cans can be melted down and reshaped into new objects, too.

You can recycle cell phones instead of letting all those metals and electronic parts go to waste in a landfill.

Planting trees helps prevent soil erosion because tree roots bind the soil together.

When humans cut down large numbers of trees, the top layer of nutrient-rich soil where plants grow is exposed. It is then more easily weathered and eroded. Planting more trees, or not cutting them down in the first place, can prevent soil erosion. In some countries farmers build walled terraces to prevent soil erosion.

The rock cycle gives us so much more than the ground beneath our feet. Remember that the next time you drink from a soda can, ride a bus, or eat an apple!

Get Smart!

Fossil fuels take millions of years to form but we are using them up rapidly. Burning fossil fuels also releases gases into Earth's atmosphere that contribute to global warming and climate change. To reduce the use of fossil fuels we need to use more renewable sources of energy, such as solar power, which uses energy from the sun to make electricity.

Glossary

atmosphere The blanket of gases that surrounds Earth.

classify To arrange things in groups according to characteristics they have in common.

core The center of Earth.

crust Earth's hard, rocky outer surface layer.

deposits Drops something down.

dissolved When a solid has broken down and seems to have disappeared into a liquid such as water.

elements Pure substances made from one type of atom. Oxygen and iron are elements.

erosion The wearing away of a rock surface. During erosion, small pieces of worn-away rock are carried from one place and deposited in another place.

fossil fuels Coal, oil, and natural gas formed from the remains of living things that died millions of years ago.

geode A spherical, hollow part in rock that is lined inside with crystals.

igneous Rock formed from magma at or below the surface of Earth.

magma Melted rock usually found beneath Earth's crust.

mantle Very deep layer of hot rock beneath Earth's crust.

metamorphic A type of rock changed from its original form by heat and/or pressure.

minerals The solid substances found naturally on Earth that make up rocks.

molten Melted.

ore A naturally occurring material that contains a metal or valuable mineral.

preserved Maintained in its original or existing state.

pressure A pushing force.

recycled Converted waste into something new.

rock cycle The process by which rocks of one kind change into rocks of another kind.

sediment Tiny pieces of rock, mud, or sand.

sedimentary A type of rock that forms when sand, stones, and other matter are pressed together over a long time.

soluble Able to be dissolved.

stalactites Hardened minerals that form icicle shapes and hang from a cave roof.

strata Layers in rock.

tectonic plates Large, moving pieces that make up Earth's outer layer.

volcanoes Openings in Earth's surface from which magma escapes from underground.

weathering The process in which rocks are broken down into tiny pieces by wind, heat, cold, rain, or moving water.

For More Information

Books

Hirsch, Rebecca E. *The Rock Cycle*. Minneapolis, MN: Core Library, 2015.

Howell, Sara. *The Rock Cycle*. New York, NY: Britannica Educational Publishing, 2018.

Lindeen, Mary. *Investigating the Rock Cycle*. Minneapolis, MN: Lerner Publications, 2016.

Oxlade, Chris. *Rocks*. Chicago, IL: Heinemann Raintree, 2016.

Watts, Pam. *The Rock Cycle*. Mankato, MN: The Child's World, 2017.

Websites

Learn more about the rock cycle at:
dkfindout.com/us/earth/rock-cycle/

Visit this website for more information on the rock cycle:
ducksters.com/science/rocks.php

Find out more and see a video about tectonic plates at:
kidsgeo.com/geology-for-kids/rock-cycle

Read more about the rock cycle and the different kinds of rock at:
www.mineralogy4kids.org/rock-cycle

Publisher's note to educators and parents: Our editors have carefully reviewed these websites to ensure that they are suitable for students. Many websites change frequently, however, and we cannot guarantee that a site's future contents will continue to meet our high standards of quality and educational value. Be advised that students should be closely supervised whenever they access the Internet.

Index

acid rain 31

crystals 5, 14–15, 25, 39

deposition 18, 29, 33

elements 5, 6
erosion 8, 9, 32–33, 34, 36, 45

fossil fuels 38, 45
fossils 20–21, 22–23

geodes 14
Giant's Causeway 15
glass 13
Grand Canyon 19

heat 6, 7, 8, 9, 10, 11, 12, 13,14, 16, 20, 24–25, 26, 27, 29

ice 30, 32, 33, 36
igneous 8, 9, 10, 11, 12–13, 14, 15, 16–17, 18, 20, 24, 26, 35

lava 12–13, 15
layers of Earth 4, 6–7, 10, 12, 14, 17, 25, 26, 27, 29
  core 6
  crust 4, 6, 12, 17, 25, 26–27, 29
  mantle 6, 7, 10, 14, 24, 26–27, 29

magma 6, 9, 10, 11, 12–13, 14, 16–17, 24
metamorphic 8, 9, 10, 11, 20, 24–25, 26–27, 28–29
minerals 4–5, 6–7, 13, 14, 18, 19, 20, 22, 25, 28, 29, 31, 34, 35, 37, 38–39, 40–41, 43, 44
  carbon 14, 41
  diamonds 14, 39
  iron 38
  metallic 40–41
    aluminum 40, 44
    copper 5, 40
    gold 5, 41, 42–43
    iron 5, 6
  silicates 5, 6, 13

nutrients 34, 36–37, 45

oceans 4, 9, 18, 24, 33
ore 41, 42–43
organic material 20, 21, 22, 23, 34, 37
  dinosaurs 20–21

pressure 6, 8, 9, 11, 12, 14, 16, 18, 20, 24, 25, 27, 38

rain 7, 19
recycling rocks 8–9, 10
rock cycle 8–9, 10–11, 12, 30, 38–39, 44–45
rock varieties 4, 13, 14, 15, 18, 25, 27, 34, 39
  basalt 13, 15
  calcite 4
  feldspar 4
  gneiss 27
  granite 4, 13, 14, 34
  limestone 4, 18, 25, 34
  marble 25
  mica 4
  obsidian 13
  pumice 13
  quartz 4, 14, 39
  slate 25, 39

sediment 8, 9, 11, 18, 19, 20, 23, 33
sedimentary 8, 9, 11, 18–19, 20, 21, 22, 23, 24, 25, 26, 27, 33
soil 34–35, 36–37, 38, 45
strata 19
surface, reaching 26–27

tectonic plates 26–27

using rocks and minerals 38–39, 40–41

volcanoes 8, 12–13, 15, 17, 26, 35

water 4, 11, 14, 18, 19, 22–23, 24, 29, 30–32, 34, 36–37
weathering 8, 9, 30–31, 33–34, 36, 38, 45
wind 30–32, 36